THE ALAMO

Mary Ann Hoffman

NEW YORK

Published in 2010 by The Rosen Publishing Group, Inc.
29 East 21st Street, New York, NY 10010

Book Design: Daniel Hosek

Photo Credits: Cover Jim Cummins/Taxi/Getty Images; pp. 3, 4, 6, 10, 12, 14, 16, 18, 22, 26, 28, 30, 31,
32 (Texas emblem on all), 3–32 (textured background), 16 (knife), 28 (monument), back cover (Texas flag)
Shutterstock.com; pp. 8, 21 courtesy Wikimedia Commons; pp. 9, 13, 24 Hulton Archive/Getty Images; p. 11
courtesy Library of Congress; p. 15 Texas State Capital, Austin, Texas; pp. 17, 25 © State Preservation Board
(2007), Austin, Texas; p. 19 courtesy Texas State Archives/The UT Institute of Texan Cultures at San Antonio;
pp. 23, 27 courtesy Center for American History, University of Texas at Austin.

Library of Congress Cataloging-in-Publication Data

Hoffman, Mary Ann, 1947-
    The Alamo / Mary Ann Hoffman.
        p. cm. — (Spotlight on Texas)
    Includes index.
    ISBN 978-1-61532-459-0 (pbk.)
    ISBN 978-1-61532-460-6 (6-pack)
    ISBN 978-1-61532-461-3 (library binding)
    1. Alamo (San Antonio, Tex.)—Juvenile literature. 2. Alamo (San Antonio, Tex.)—Siege, 1836—Juvenile
literature. 3. Texas—History—To 1846—Juvenile literature. 4. San Antonio (Tex.)—Buildings, structures,
etc.—Juvenile literature. I. Title.
    F390.H597 2010
    976.4′03—dc22
                                2009032279

Manufactured in the United States of America

CPSIA Compliance Information: Batch # WW10RC: For further information contact Rosen Publishing, New York, New York at 1-800-237-9932.

CONTENTS

A Spanish Claim

In 1519, Spanish explorer Alonso Álvarez de Pineda was the first European to reach Texas. Other Spanish **explorers** followed. They claimed the land for Spain. However, Spain wasn't interested in settling the area. In 1685, French explorers founded a settlement on the coast of the Gulf of Mexico. The Spanish decided to guard their claim to the territory. They set up **missions** to spread the Spanish way of life to Native Americans. They also sent soldiers to stop other countries from claiming land in "New Spain."

In 1718, a mission was built along the San Antonio River. It was called San Antonio de Valero. In 1803, Spanish soldiers from Mexico moved into the mission. They were likely the first to call it the "Alamo."

This picture shows how the Alamo in San Antonio, Texas, looks today. Some people say it was named after the cottonwood trees that grew nearby. *Alamo* is the Spanish word for "cottonwood."

MEXICAN TEXAS

Since the first Spanish explorers arrived, Texas had been part of New Spain. Mexico was also part of New Spain. Mexico's people grew unhappy with Spanish rule. They wanted to govern themselves. In 1821, Mexico finally won its independence and gained control of much of Texas.

Mexico's government wanted more people living in Texas. They granted land to U.S. citizens who promised to settle there. At first, these **Anglo** settlers were allowed to govern themselves. They could choose their leaders and form **militias**.

The "Father of Texas"

In 1821, Moses Austin of Missouri received a land grant from the Mexican government. After his death later that year, his son Stephen founded the first Anglo settlement in Texas. Stephen Austin was the leader of the settlement of about 300 families. He wrote laws and helped set up schools, roads, and businesses. Some call him the "father of Texas."

In this map from 1821, much of Texas is labeled "Great Space of Land unknown."

Mexican leaders became concerned that more Anglos than Mexicans were living in Texas. They increased government control over the area. In 1830, the Mexican government banned more U.S. settlement in Texas. Texas and another Mexican state were combined into a single state called Coahuila (koh-ah-WEE-lah) and Texas. The capital was moved farther into Mexico.

These changes made settlers angry. In 1833, Stephen Austin went to Mexico City to talk with President Antonio López de Santa Anna. Angered by Austin's message from the settlers, Santa Anna put him in prison. He also took power away from all local governments in Texas.

Texans talked of breaking away from Mexico. Mexican soldiers and Texas settlers began fighting in 1835. Texas leaders signed a **declaration** of independence on March 2, 1836.

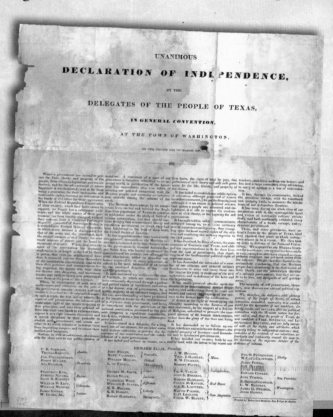

Santa Anna didn't believe Mexico was ready for a government ruled by the people. He named himself dictator, which is a ruler with total control of a country.

THE REVOLUTION

The small town of Gonzales became the first major battlefield of the Texas **Revolution**. The Mexican government had given the town a **cannon** to guard itself against Native American attacks. Santa Anna sent troops to Gonzales to take back the cannon. The people of the town forced the troops to leave without the cannon.

After Stephen Austin was freed from his Mexican prison, he returned to Texas ready to fight. In December 1835, Austin led a group of **volunteers** in an attack against Mexican troops at the Alamo. The Mexicans left, and about 100 Texans moved into the mission. An angry Santa Anna sent more troops into Texas.

the cannon of Gonzales, Texas

Mexican soldier José Juan Sánchez Navarro made this drawing of the Alamo. It was made in the mid-1830s and is the earliest picture of the building.

SAMUEL HOUSTON

Samuel Houston, often called "Sam," moved to Texas in 1832. He quickly became a leader. By 1835, he believed that Texans should fight for their freedom. In 1836, Texas officials chose Houston to be the head of the Texas army.

Houston knew the army needed more soldiers. Three days after Texans took back the Alamo, Houston called for volunteers.

Famous Texan, Famous American

Sam Houston is considered by many to be a famous Texan. However, he was born in Virginia and lived for many years in Tennessee. Houston was 39 years old when he moved to Texas.

Houston had a full life. He was a military hero in the Texas Revolution. He's the only person in U.S. history to have been the governor of two states—Tennessee and Texas. Houston was also the president of the **Republic** of Texas twice and a U.S. senator for Texas.

CHARACTER

- brave
- leader
- daring
- hardworking
- dependable

Sam Houston

ACTIONS

- looked for adventure
- supported freedom
- fought for independence
- commanded the army
- led the Republic of Texas

DAVID CROCKETT

A man born in Tennessee answered Houston's call for volunteers. David "Davy" Crockett was famous throughout the United States as an adventurous hero. He was skilled with guns. He could also track and hunt wild animals. He was known as a man who could live in wild, unsettled territory. Crockett was a **legend** in his own time. In the 1800s, he was the subject of books, cartoons, drawings, and paintings.

Crockett's fame helped him enter government. He won election to the Tennessee **legislature** and the U.S. Congress. In 1835, he lost an election. He moved to Texas in 1836. By February 8, 1836, he had joined other Texas independence fighters at the Alamo.

In this painting, Crockett's clothes show his pride as a hunter. He called his gun "Betsy."

James Bowie

James "Jim" Bowie was another man who joined the fight against Mexico. Like Crockett, Bowie was a legendary **frontiersman**. He was said to have ridden wild alligators! He moved to Texas looking for adventure and riches.

After Santa Anna took power, Bowie formed a militia and worked with Houston's army. In January 1836, Sam Houston asked Bowie and some of his men to go to the Alamo. Some people say he was supposed to tear it down. However, Bowie decided to stay and guard the mission from Santa Anna's forces. He became the leader of the volunteers at the Alamo.

A Special Knife

Jim Bowie was known for his fighting ability with a knife. He used a special knife that was first made for his brother. A Bowie knife has a long, wide blade with a curved point and a guard to keep the user's hand safe. The knife became so famous that classes were taught on how to use it. Bowie knives were even made in England.

A friend described Bowie as a man whom "no one dared to undervalue and many feared."

WILLIAM B. TRAVIS

William Barret Travis commanded the Texas army at the Alamo. He was born in South Carolina in 1809 and grew up in Alabama. He became a lawyer and even started a newspaper. In 1831, Travis moved to Texas and set up a law practice. He learned to speak Spanish so that he could talk with the Mexicans.

Travis was an early supporter of Texas independence. He joined the Texas militia and then the army. He was among those who began the **siege** to force the Mexican troops from the Alamo. In 1836, Travis was ordered to gather 100 men and return to San Antonio. He could only gather twenty-nine men. He thought this was too few men, so he asked to be excused from his duty. However, his orders remained.

William Travis traveled to fight at Gonzales in October 1835. He arrived after the battle was over.

Travis reached the Alamo on February 3, 1836. He was named the new commander. Jim Bowie and his volunteers were already there. Travis and Bowie argued about who was in charge. Finally, they agreed Travis would command the army. Bowie took command of all volunteers.

Santa Anna and the Mexican army began a siege of the Alamo on February 23, 1836. Travis knew he needed more men since he had fewer than 200. On February 24, he sent a letter titled "To the People of Texas and All Americans in the World." It appeared in newspapers on March 2 and 5. Travis wrote of the experience of the siege at the Alamo and the need for more soldiers. Many men volunteered, but none reached the Alamo in time.

This sign shows Travis's letter. Some of his words have become famous: "I shall never surrender or retreat." He meant that he would never give up or run away from the Mexican forces.

LETTER FROM THE ALAMO.

COMMANDANCY OF THE ALAMO-
BEXAR, FEBY. 24 TH 1836-
TO THE PEOPLE OF TEXAS & ALL AMERICANS IN THE WORLD--

FELLOW CITIZENS & COMPATRIOTS
I AM BESIEGED, BY A THOUSAND OR MORE OF THE MEXICANS AND SANTA ANNA- I HAVE SUSTAINED A CONTINUAL BOMBARDMENT & CANNONADE FOR 24 HOURS & HAVE NOT LOST A MAN- THE ENEMY HAS DEMANDED A SURRENDER AT DISCRETION, OTHERWISE, THE GARRISON ARE TO BE PUT TO THE SWORD, IF THE FORT IS TAKEN- I HAVE ANSWERED THE DEMAND WITH A CANNON SHOT, & OUR FLAG STILL WAVES PROUDLY FROM THE WALLS- I SHALL NEVER SURRENDER OR RETREAT THEN, I CALL ON YOU IN THE NAME OF LIBERTY, OF PATRIOTISM & EVERYTHING DEAR TO THE AMERICAN CHARACTER TO COME TO OUR AID, WITH ALL DISPATCH - THE ENEMY IS RECEIVING REINFORCEMENTS DAILY AND WILL NO DOUBT INCREASE TO THREE OR FOUR THOUSAND IN FOUR OR FIVE DAYS.
IF THIS CALL IS NEGLECTED, I AM DETERMINED TO SUSTAIN MYSELF AS LONG AS POSSIBLE & DIE LIKE A SOLDIER WHO NEVER FORGETS WHAT IS DUE TO HIS OWN HONOR & THAT OF HIS COUNTRY- VICTORY OR DEATH

WILLIAM BARRET TRAVIS
LT. COL. COMDT.

P.S. THE LORD IS ON OUR SIDE- WHEN THE ENEMY APPEARED IN SIGHT WE HAD NOT THREE BUSHELS OF CORN- WE HAVE SINCE FOUND IN DESERTED HOUSES 80 OR 90 BUSHELS & GOT INTO THE WALLS 20 OR 30 HEAD OF BEEVES-

TRAVIS

21

THE BATTLE

The Mexican army had a steady supply of men and **ammunition**. They could get more if needed. The people inside the Alamo were surrounded. They had only the supplies that were there when the siege began. Still, they held off the Mexican forces for 13 days. They remained hopeful more men would come to help them.

The Alamo had walkways near the tops of the walls. These allowed the men inside to fire over the walls. However, they also made it easier for the Mexicans to see and shoot at the men inside. Santa Anna carefully studied the building and observed each day's events. He believed the men in the Alamo were running low on ammunition and supplies. He waited for the right moment to attack.

José Juan Sánchez Navarro made this 1836 battle map of the Alamo for Santa Anna. The letters "R" and "V" show where the Mexican soldiers placed their cannons.

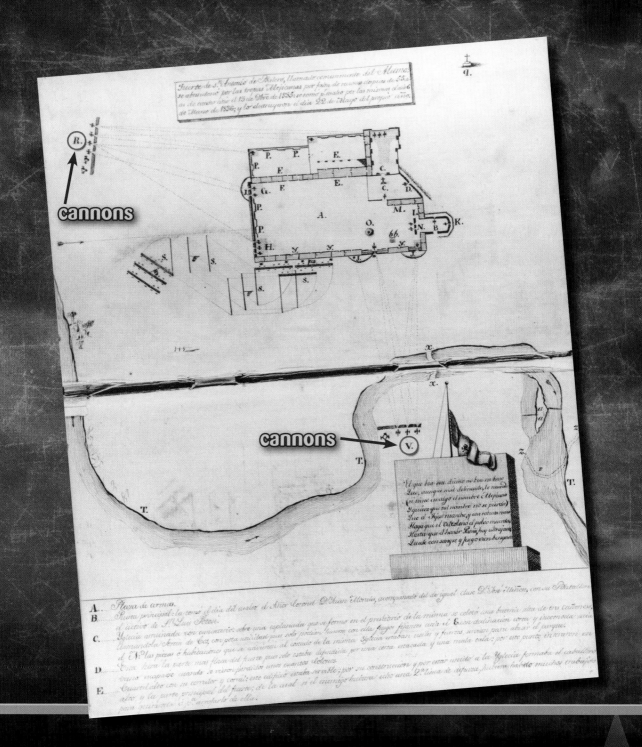

cannons

cannons

23

Some say that when the Alamo fighters ran out of bullets, they used their guns as clubs. This painting shows David Crockett (left center) doing this as he fights the Mexicans inside the Alamo.

In the early morning of March 6, 1836, Santa Anna's men attacked the Alamo. At first, the men inside kept them out. However, there were too many Mexican soldiers. Santa Anna's troops regrouped several times. They continued the attack until they could climb the walls. William Travis was among the first to die.

The Alamo fighters then moved farther inside the mission. This allowed the Mexicans to get over the walls. Once the Mexicans were inside, they battled the Alamo fighters hand to hand. Bowie, who had been ill, was killed in his bed. The Battle of the Alamo lasted only about an hour and a half.

Dawn at the Alamo (1905 painting)

SURVIVORS

Santa Anna ordered that no Alamo fighters be left alive. The few men who had survived the battle were immediately killed. Some think David Crockett was one of these.

The Alamo survivors included women, children, and slaves. One story tells that Santa Anna gave each survivor a blanket and money before he let them go. Santa Anna wanted these people to tell others the story of the Alamo. He wanted the people of Texas to fear the Mexican army. He wanted them to think that independence was impossible. Instead, Texans became very angry. The cry "Remember the Alamo!" made them want to win independence even more.

Angelina Dickinson (shown here) and her mother, Susanna, were among the Alamo survivors. Angelina was just a baby at that time.

Angelina Dickinson

THE LEGEND

The story of the Alamo soon grew into a famous legend. The Alamo is a story of independence, bravery, and the strength to fight for a cause. It's said that "Remember the Alamo!" was heard at the Battle of San Jacinto on April 21, 1836. Sam Houston and his soldiers brought down Santa Anna's army in under half an hour! This battle ended the Texas Revolution. Texas became an independent republic.

This monument, called Heroes of the Alamo, stands in front of the Texas capitol building in Austin, Texas.

A Timeline of the Alamo During the Texas Revolution

December 1835	Texans take Alamo from Mexicans.
January 1836	Samuel Houston sends James Bowie to Alamo.
February 3, 1836	William B. Travis arrives at Alamo.
February 8, 1836	David Crockett comes to Alamo.
February 23, 1836	Santa Anna and his soldiers begin siege.
February 24, 1836	William Travis sends letter for help.
March 2 and 5, 1836	Newspapers print Travis's letter.
March 6, 1836	Attack on Alamo begins and ends in one and a half hours.
April 21, 1836	"Remember the Alamo!" is heard at Battle of San Jacinto.

READER RESPONSE PROJECTS

- Look at the character/actions map on page 13. Complete a character/actions map about the person from this book that you find most interesting. Use what you have read, the Internet, and your library to help you learn more about the person.

- The Battle of the Alamo is considered a major part of the history of Texas and the United States. To many people, this battle is more famous than the Battle of San Jacinto that ended the war. Write two or three paragraphs telling why you think this is.

- Use the facts in this book to help you create a poster of the Battle of the Alamo. Use words and pictures you think best tell the story of the events that occurred at the mission. Display your poster in the classroom.

- Use pictures in this book and other resources to build a model of the Alamo before or after the battle. After your work is completed, show your class the model. Be prepared to answer questions about the battle and your work.

GLOSSARY

ammunition (am-yuh-NIH-shun) Things fired from guns, such as bullets.

Anglo (AN-gloh) A white, non-Hispanic person from the United States.

cannon (KA-nuhn) A large, heavy gun that is usually on wheels.

declaration (deh-kluh-RAY-shun) An official announcement.

explorer (ihk-SPLOHR-uhr) Someone who travels to find new lands.

frontiersman (fruhn-TIHRZ-muhn) A man who lives or works on the edge of settled land.

legend (LEH-juhnd) A story that is widely believed but cannot be proven.

legislature (LEH-juhs-lay-chur) A group of people with the power to make or pass laws.

militia (muh-LIH-shuh) A group of ordinary people who are not soldiers but are trained and ready to fight when needed.

mission (MIH-shun) A place where church leaders teach their beliefs and help the community.

republic (rih-PUH-blihk) A form of government in which the people elect the leaders who run the government.

revolution (reh-vuh-LOO-shun) A complete change in government brought about by force.

siege (SEEJ) Blocking off a fort or city with soldiers so that nothing can get in or go out.

volunteer (vah-luhn-TIHR) Someone who fights in a war but is not a member of the regular army.

INDEX

Due to the changing nature of Internet links, the Rosen Publishing Group, Inc., has developed an online list of Web sites related to the subject of this book. This site is updated regularly. Please use this link to access the list: **http://www.rcbmlinks.com/sot/alamo/**